WOODLAND
WILDLIFE

Rabbits

by G. G. Lake

raintree
a Capstone company — publishers for children

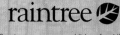

Pebble
Plus

Raintree is an imprint of Capstone Global Library Limited, a company incorporated in England and Wales having its registered office at 264 Banbury Road, Oxford, OX2 7DY – Registered company number: 6695582

www.raintree.co.uk
myorders@raintree.co.uk

Edited by Gena Chester
Designed by Juliette Peters
Picture research by Wanda Winch
Production by Steve Walker
Printed and bound in China

ISBN 978 1 4747 2184 4 (hardback)
20 19 18 17 16
10 9 8 7 6 5 4 3 2 1

ISBN 978 1 4747 2187 5 (paperback)
21 20 19 18 17
10 9 8 7 6 5 4 3 2 1

British Library Cataloguing in Publication Data
A full catalogue record for this book is available from the British Library.

Acknowledgements
We would like to thank the following for permission to reproduce photographs: Dreamstime: Alberttr, 9 (top); iStockphoto, bradwieland, 11, MidwestWilderness, 19; Minden Pictures: FLPA/Paul Sawer, 13, NPL/Kim Taylor, 17; Shutterstock: alicedaniel, illustrated forest items, Anna Subbotina, 22–23, AR Pictures, tree bark design, Berents, 21, D and D Photo Sudbury, cover, elina, 24, Jack Dean III, 5, LorraineHudgins, 15, mythja, 1, Ron Rowan Photography, 7, Stawek, 9 (map), Sunny Forest, 3

Every effort has been made to contact copyright holders of material reproduced in this book. Any omissions will be rectified in subsequent printings if notice is given to the publisher.

Printed and bound in China.

Contents

Speedy hoppers

A rabbit races through the wood. Powerful back legs help the rabbit to hop quickly. It dashes into its underground home.

All rabbits have long ears.

Wild rabbits' ears stick straight up.

Their ears hear sounds

from far away.

7

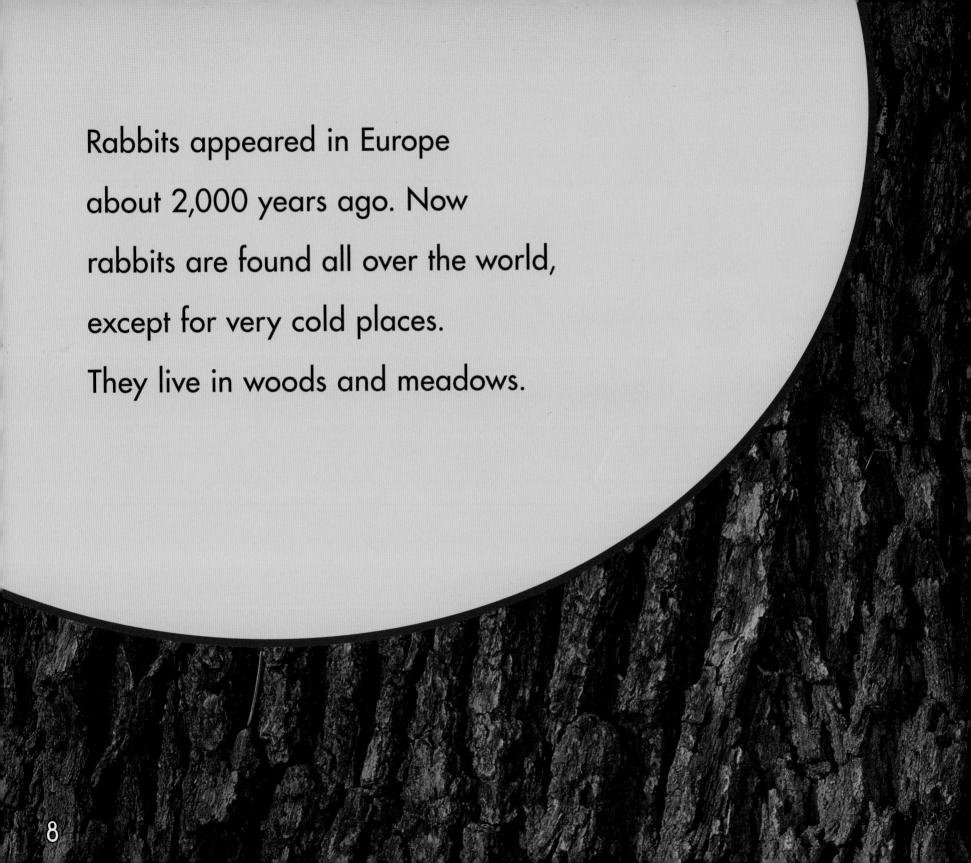

Rabbits appeared in Europe
about 2,000 years ago. Now
rabbits are found all over the world,
except for very cold places.
They live in woods and meadows.

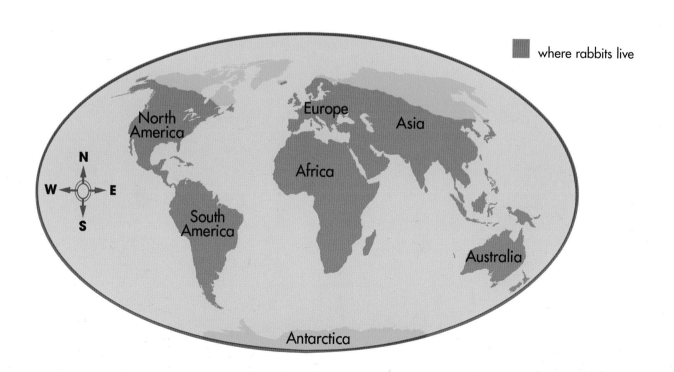

where rabbits live

North America

Europe

Asia

Africa

South America

Australia

Antarctica

N
W E
S

Woodland homes

Homes keep rabbits safe from danger.

Some rabbits live on the ground

in nests. Nests are made

from rabbit fur and grass.

Most rabbits dig holes to live in. These underground holes are called burrows. A warren is made up of several burrows connected by tunnels.

Food

Rabbits eat grass, weeds, fruit and vegetables. Their long teeth help them to break up their food.

Staying safe

Rabbits have many predators.

They stay safe by listening.

Their ears hear the softest of sounds.

If they sense danger, they run away.

Baby rabbits

Baby rabbits are called kittens.

A mother can give birth four

to five times a year. She has

about five kittens each time.

Kittens are born blind and hairless.

The kittens leave home after a few weeks. In three months, they have grown up. Wild rabbits live for up to four years.

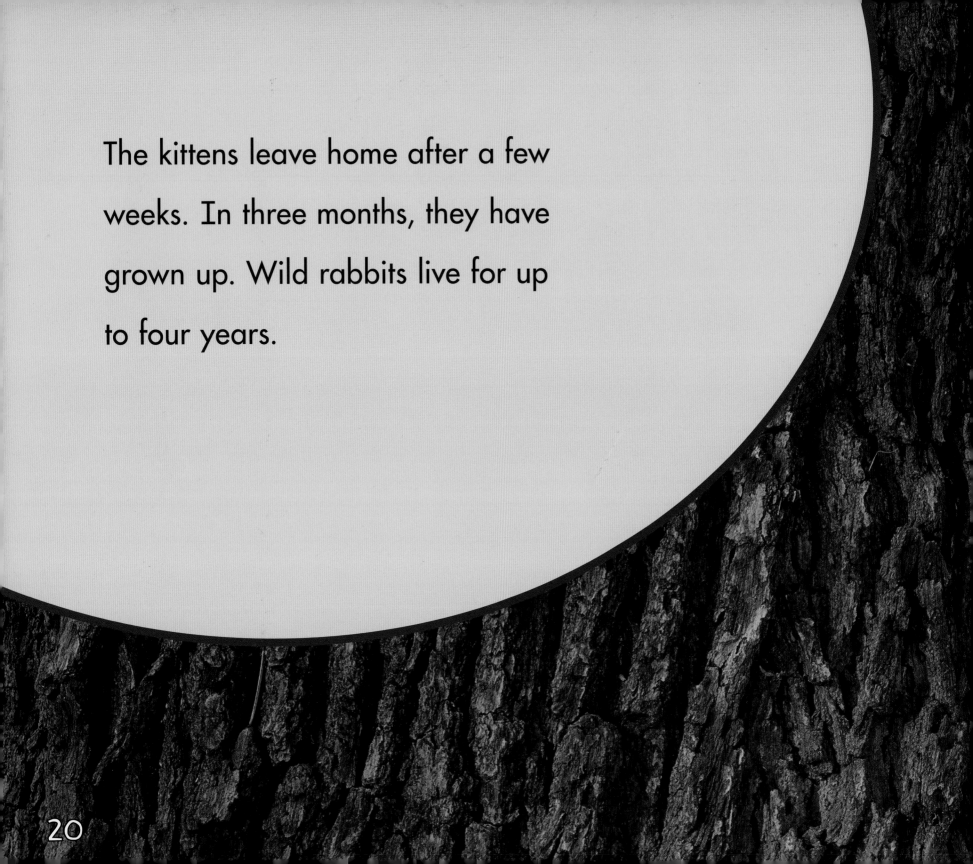

Glossary

blind unable to see or having very limited sight

burrow hole in the ground made or used by an animal

fur thick hair that covers an animal

kitten young rabbit

meadow big, low area of land that is covered in grass

nest home of insects, birds or other animals

predator animal that hunts other animals for food

warren underground burrow system connected by tunnels; rabbits build warrens for safety and sleeping

wild in its natural state

Read more

A Nature Walk in the Woods (Nature Walks), Louise and Richard Spilsbury (Raintree, 2015)

Learning About Animals (The Natural World), Catherine Veitch (Raintree, 2014)

Look Inside a Burrow (Look Inside a...), Richard and Louise Spilsbury (Raintree, 2014)

Websites

www.bbc.co.uk/nature/life/Leporidae
Discover more about wild hares and rabbits.

www.wildlifetrusts.org/species/rabbit
Find out more about wild rabbits, including when and where to spot them!

Comprehension questions

1. Where in the world do rabbits live?

2. What makes up a warren?

3. How do rabbits stay safe from predators?

Index